OHIO

OHIO

by Art Weber

PRESS, INC.

Minocqua, Wisconsin

DEDICATION

To my wonderful sons Andy and Brian,
whose boundless energy and curiosity helps me see the world through youthful eyes.
And to Pat, whose love and support made this book possible.

©Art Weber, 1995

Photography ©Art Weber, 1995: 12 (top), 14-15, 18, 20, 23 (both), 24, 25, 32-33, 34-35, 36, 37, 40-41, 46, 47, 48, 54, 58, 61, 72, 77, 82 (both), 83, 84, 100-101, 104, 106, 107, 108-109, 113, 114, 116, 124, 127. ©Dembinsky Photo Associates, 1995: Sharon Cummings: 73, 78; Doug Locke: 76; Skip Moody 12 (inset), 42, 50, 88-89, 118; Bill Lea: 63, 102, 117; Gary Mesaros: 2, 13, 26-27, 30, 39, 51, 66, 75, 103, 110, 111, 119; Adam Jones: Back cover; Jim Roetzel: 123; Carl R. Sams II: 19, 74; Stan Osolinski: 22. G. Alan Nelson: 98; George E. Stewart: 10, 92 (left); Dick Scott: 92 (inset). ©Jerry Sieve, 1995: Front cover, 6-7, 8-9, 17, 28-29, 31, 43, 44, 52-53, 55, 56-57, 62, 64-65, 67, 68-69, 71, 79, 80-81, 87, 90, 93, 94-95, 97, 120-121, 128, Front cover flap.

NorthWord Press, Inc.
P.O. Box 1360
Minocqua, WI 54548

Book design by Lisa Moore

Library of Congress Cataloging-in-Publication Data

Weber, Art.
        Wild Ohio / by Art Weber.
                p.   cm.
        ISBN 1-55971-437-5 (hc)
        1. Natural history—Ohio. 2. Physical geography—Ohio.
I. Title.
QH105.03W435 1995
        508.771—dc20   95-14868

Printed in Mexico

ACKNOWLEDGMENTS

Where does one start when acknowledging all those who made this book possible? Do I start with my parents who instilled the love of nature and beauty; with my Uncle Wallie and Aunt Irene whose love of the outdoors, travel and photography shaped my view of the world; with Mark, Tim, Joe, Chris and Jon, childhood friends who shared countless hours in the woods and fields observing and pursuing nature? Or do I start with Steve Pollick, Outdoors Editor of *The* (Toledo) *Blade*, who for so long has been my great friend, cheerleader and sounding board? Or Jim DuFresne, outdoor writer extraordinaire and author of *Wild Michigan*, who suggested this book for me?

It's a given that acknowledgments can't be done without leaving out someone important who should share the credit. To that person or those people I apologize in advance and make the offer of buying a beverage at the tavern of choice to, if not make up for the oversight, renew conversation and friendship.

The book simply could not have been done without Pat, my wife, travel companion and biggest booster. Nor without the cooperation and understanding of my sons, Andy and Brian, and step-children, Christopher and Ashley.

My co-workers at Metroparks of the Toledo Area were instrumental. First, my friend and boss, Jean Ward, for his support and understanding; Joe Croy, my go-to guru when the questions seemed unanswerable and the manuscript needed review; and to Michelle Grigore for her staccato of ideas and information that fueled the contents of the book.

How can I properly thank John O'Meara, director of Geauga County Parks, for his valued friendship and for opening my eyes to the beauty of Northeast Ohio? Or Helen and Peter O'Meara for their wonderful hospitality?

Immeasurable thanks to Jim Bissell of the Cleveland Museum of Natural History for his good-humored patience in the virtually impossible mission of distilling his unparalleled knowledge of the Ohio landscape for my eager consumption. Similar accolades go to Chris Bedel of the Cincinnati Museum of Natural History who so willingly introduced me to the spectacular Edge of Appalachia. And to Steve McKee, director of Gorman Nature Center, for sharing a morning in Fowler Woods State Nature Preserve.

Of the many agencies that lent a hand it is Ohio's Division of Natural Areas and Preserves that stands above the rest. I can't bestow enough compliments on Division Chief and fellow native Toledoan Guy Denny, Jennifer Windus, Nancy Strayer, Phil Zito, Bill Hudson, Jim McCormac and so many others both for the important and good work they do for all Ohioans and for their unhesitating and unfailing cooperation. I only hope this book does justice to the beauty of their mission.

There, too, were the Ohio Division of Wildlife, especially Mark Shieldcastle; Ohio State Parks, and State Forests. Mark and Julie Shieldcastle deserve recognition both as great friends and in their visionary roles in the Black Swamp Bird Observatory.

Kudos, too, to Rita Jones of the Hocking Tourism Association for her wonderful and patient cooperation. Ditto for Bob Eulas of the Lake County Convention Bureau, Melinda Huntley of the Sandusky/Erie County Visitors and Convention Bureau, Sue Ayers and Jean Lucas of the Cambridge/Guernsey County Convention Bureau, Mary Hall of the Portsmouth Convention and Visitor Bureau, and Lee Tasseff of Richland Travel and Tourism.

Many thanks to the Amerihost Inn in Logan and managers Candy Bradley and Valerie Junge, to Jim Gould of the Holiday Inn in Cambridge, to Jeanette Henry of the HoJo Inn in Norwalk, and to the Atwood Lodge operated by the Muskingum Watershed Conservancy District. And thanks to Lon Huffman, Coachmen Industries, Inc., for the van camper which proved its worth repeatedly on the tough roads of southern Ohio.

And to Harold Mayfield, the man who knows so much more than I.

. . . beautiful Ohio, in dreams again I see visions of what used to be . . .
—from "Beautiful Ohio," Ohio's official song

There's no need to dream about what used to be in Ohio. Wild Ohio is alive and doing pretty well, all things considered.

Ohioans are fiercely proud of their natural heritage. Ohio's seventy-eight state parks are among the most heavily visited in the nation. A number of the state's eighty-eight counties have established Metropark systems which maintain an extensive array of natural area parks. Additional acres are set aside in state nature preserves, state forests and the Wayne National Forest, in state wildlife areas, in the units of the Ottawa National Wildlife Refuge, by the Muskingum Watershed Conservancy District, in the properties of the Ohio Nature Conservancy, the Ohio Historical Society, the Cleveland Museum of Natural History and the Cincinnati Museum of Natural History. Wild Ohio is every-where for those who take the time to see it.

Ohio is a tremendously diverse state, blessed with nature's bounty. That bounty is reflected in the richness of Ohio's wetlands, forests and prairies. It is in the deep, fertile soils of Ohio's cropland and the volume of fresh water held in huge lakes, countless streams and in massive underground aquifers.

Nature has even defined much of the state's borders with a great lake to the north and a great river to the south and southeast. Between these natural

boundaries are lake plains and Appalachian foothills, bogs and cliffs, and the plants and animals unique to each.

When you come to Ohio, though, don't expect breathtaking views rivaling the scale of the Great West. Awesome vistas are hard to come by. Part of the problem is that Ohio, especially southeast Ohio, is still heavily forested; all those darn trees block the view. So, stop trying to look past the trees. Drop your eyes, focus them closer. The beauty of Ohio is not in vistas, but in its wondrous intricacy, its marvelous variety.

True enough, the bountiful natural area that the first European settlers found when they made their way into what was then part of the Northwest Territories has changed. The scale is gone. Too late we've come to understand the value of wetlands. Most of them are gone. Though trees still cover large parts of the state, they have been heavily timbered. Many have been cut over twice, some three or four times. An alarming number of the state's streams are heavily silted with agricultural run-off. In many ways, Ohio is no different from any other state. There are landfills that leak, industries that pollute.

Still, Wild Ohio not just survives, it thrives where it has been left to its own devices.

I once asked a man much wiser than I, a naturalist and ornithologist of international renown, to compare the Alaskan wilderness with Ohio. His answer bears reading and rereading until it is in our heads—that the natural

area right down the street can be as rich and fascinating as the celebrated wilderness we view on television.

"Wildlife depends on the fertility of the soil," he said, "and ultimately the fertility of the soil determines the amount of life—both plant and animal. So this region was much richer and is much richer even today where land is left in a natural state, much richer than anything to be found in Alaska. The attraction of Alaska is that it is in its natural state, it has not been much changed. The big mammals which can't live in a civilized or densely populated area still live up there because of the vast open stretches. If you count the number of animals per square mile it's not nearly as much there as here."

Wild Ohio is a personal celebration of a wonderful land. It is not, by any standards, a textbook. It is meant to be an appetizer, an invitation, to see Ohio in a new way. Let this book open a door to new adventures. Enjoy Wild Ohio, see all its faces, see it in all seasons, savor its beauty. Come to that primal understanding of how inextricably tied we all are to the earth. Then step forward and speak for it.

Marshes of the Western Basin

or thousands of years Lake Erie worked its magic unhindered by the hand of man.

It sloshed life-giving water over a half-million acres around Maumee Bay and the lake's western basin. Water so clear and clean that acre upon acre of wild rice waved in the wind at untold numbers of waterfowl. Marsh and swamp stretched inland as far as the eye could see.

Today we call them wetlands, the transition between dry land and open water that is both land and water, yet neither. They were strange and wonderful places, these wetlands, incredibly rich and diverse. Water and land combined in a primordial-like soup where countless life forms are nurtured.

Few places are as level as Lake Erie's western basin. Credit the Wisconsin glacier which ground down out of the north like a gigantic earthmover doing the rough grading work. A succession of prehistoric lakes larger than present-day Lake Erie did the finish grading, smoothing the area billiard table flat. So flat that even small increases in lake levels could change large expanses of dry land to wet.

With settlement came farm tiles and ditches to drain the marshes and swamps and, later, fortress-like dikes to hold back a lake that constantly sought to reclaim the land. The swamps were logged and the marshes drained revealing the fertile topsoil to farming.

Today's marshes are pinned between the moody lake and encroaching civilization. Ironically, the dikes that tame the lake are also crucial to the survival of the remaining marshes. The most productive and the most natural marshes are those protected by dikes that stifle destructive wave action and enable managers to precisely control water levels.

The sheer scale is gone, only a fraction of those original marshes remain. But the Lake Erie marshes of modern Ohio are still strange, wonderful and diverse. The best of what's left is protected in a handful of federal, state and private marshes: the units of the Ottawa National Wildlife Refuge; Magee Marsh, home of the Ohio Division of Wildlife's Crane Creek Waterfowl Experiment Station; Pickerel Creek Wildlife Area on Sandusky Bay; and the holdings of several private waterfowl clubs.

Preceding page: Ohio's
wetlands are among the
richest anywhere, especially
the marshes of the western
basin of Lake Erie.

Right: Sunset, Ottawa National Wildlife Refuge.

Land of the Eagle

There aren't many trees in a marsh—there aren't supposed to be. Just expanses of cattails, bulrushes, arrowhead, lotus and pickerelweed interrupted by watery openings engineered by the beaver of the marsh, the muskrat.

Here and there, where the land rises just enough out of the wet, is a tree, usually a cottonwood. They grow fast, grow big, die young and stand like skeletons, bare and alone. Perfect sentinel posts for the master of the marsh, the bald eagle.

From these open perches, the bald eagle surveys its domain. It is a sea eagle, really, interested mostly in feeding on fish but if the pickings are easy it sometimes turns to waterfowl, small mammals and—unbefitting its regal image—carrion. Except in the coldest depths of winter, the eagle is there. It claims the marsh and protects it as its own, defending it from intrusion even of its own offspring returning home after a nomadic youth.

In January, when winter still holds its icy grip on the marsh, the eagle and its mate are renewing ties to their nest, a nest that may have been used for a decade or more. Each year they add material, sticks and twigs for stability; grasses, cattails and corn stalks for softer bedding. Their nests are always large, sometimes gargantuan. The largest nest ever recorded, the "Great Nest" in Vermilion, Ohio, was used by a succession of eagle pairs over thirty-five years. Eighty feet up in an old shagbark hickory tree, it measured twelve feet deep and well over eight feet wide when it finally plummeted to the ground in a vicious late winter storm in 1925.

Right: The bald eagle's once uncertain future in Ohio is now secure. From a perilous low of only four nesting pairs in the 1970s, eagle nests now occupy virtually all of the prime western basin habitat. Younger eagles are now drifting farther and farther into Ohio's interior, establishing nesting territories well into central Ohio.

Left: Immature black-crowned night heron, Cedar Point National Wildlife Refuge.

By March, with the marsh still locked in ice, the eagle and its mate are incubating their clutch of two, sometimes three, eggs.

Even in winter the marsh is alive. Canada geese, mallard and black ducks, herring and ring-billed gulls keep small pools open most of the winter. Muskrats escape their cattail cabins and move under the ice to food caches. Fox and mink make their nocturnal rounds. Offshore, in open pockets of the lake and bay, merganser and scaup raft in huge numbers.

In spring the eagle witnesses hundreds of thousands of birds—ducks and divers, egrets and herons, hawks and songbirds—moving in and moving on. Located at an intersection of the Atlantic and Mississippi flyways, the western basin is not only an important nesting site, but one of North America's most important refueling stops for northward-bound birds. It is a kaleidoscope of color and action, made all the more obvious by the unobstructed view across the marsh.

The early green growth that barely showed in the April marsh grows thick and seemingly impenetrable by June, concealing the activities of parents raising their young. Life in the summer marsh takes on a different tone. Warblers and other songbirds which filled the marsh with song in spring while mating and establishing territories have become more reclusive and taken a lower profile as security from predators.

On the eagle's nest, the young are as large as their parents, jumping about and exercising newly feathered wings. By July they will take their first awkward flights dressed in rich brown plumage. It will be several years before they sport the distinctive white head and tail of a mature bald eagle. Their early fledging is fortuitous. The young eagles will perfect their hunting skills in the easy days of summer and fall when prey is plentiful.

Ohio enjoys huge flocks of both migrating and resident Canada geese. The giant race of Canada geese, once thought extinct, has rebounded in Ohio and can now be found throughout the state. Nowhere is their return more apparent than at Ottawa National Wildlife Refuge and neighboring Magee Marsh State Wildlife Area.

Undercover

Heard but unseen in the cattails and pickerelweed are grebes, coots and gallinules. Ducks from mallards to teal to woodies are here, too. It is the females that stay with the young, the males often departing before incubation is complete. Good cover is important to both mother and brood. She is molting and flightless while the young are only beginning to grow their flight feathers.

Temporarily flightless, too, are the Canada geese. Male and female form strong pair bonds, establish long-term territories and fiercely defend their broods.

Today there are plenty of broods of the giant race of Canada geese to defend, but not so long ago the race was considered extinct. Rediscovered in the upper midwest some forty years ago, the giant Canada goose population was revived using management techniques developed at the Crane Creek Waterfowl Experiment Station.

Marsh wrens and red-winged blackbirds are among the songbirds that find nesting sites in the middle of the marsh. Common yellowthroats, prothonotary warblers, yellow warblers, indigo buntings, Traill's flycatchers and swamp sparrows are among those that prefer sites in the brush and treelines along the edge.

Left: A nesting sandhill crane is a fairly rare sight in Ohio.

Inset: The Blandings turtle is common to area marshes.

Right: Great egret, Ottawa National Wildlife Refuge.

As summer wears on, water levels drop, exposing mudflats favored by shorebirds. Dunlins, short-billed dowitchers, sanderlings, semipalmated sandpipers and least sandpipers are some of the more conspicuous species.

Most ubiquitous, though, are the herons, seemingly countless great blue herons, great egrets and black-crowned night herons. On the dead-calm evenings of summer when the insects are humming and the "jug o'rum" call of the bullfrog is echoing, the herons gather, silhouetted against a red ball sunset soon to be extinguished in the placid lake waters. Black-crowned night herons startle the scene with their loud, throaty, "kwanks," signifying the arrival of the night shift.

By September, waterfowl and warblers are making their way south again from northern nesting grounds. By October, a single marsh can blacken with birds.

School's out for the young-of-the-year eagles. They are on their own now, joining with the other immature eagles who have not yet staked out territory. They are nomads, moving southward for the winter and who-knows-where for the coming summer and beyond. If they survive, instincts will eventually bring them back to the land of the eagle.

But before they go, there is time for games. The young eagles gather—two, three, maybe four at a time—in the skies above the marsh. They dive at each other, the mock prey flipping at the last instant showing talons grown strong and deadly. They cartwheel and cavort in aerial displays, at once showing off speed, strength, grace and beauty. The games hone their skills, preparing them for a life on their own.

Then they are gone. The mature eagles stay on, surveying their territory from a lofty perch in an old, dead cottonwood.

Left: Arrowhead is a common—and easily recognizable—plant of the western basin marshes. Though the distinctive leaves give the plant its name, it is the tubers produced in the marsh muck that give it its nickname, "duck potatoes," which are eaten by ducks and other animals of the marsh.

Right: American lotus seed pods and leaves, Old Man's Creek.

Following page: Waterfowl on Lake Erie, Lorain Harbor.

OAK OPENINGS

It is a fluke of geology and geography that a narrow band of sandy soil just west of Toledo comprises one of earth's rarest habitats.

Here the great hardwood forests to the east meet and mingle with the expansive tall-grass prairies to the west, forming a very different kind of habitat that locals call the Oak Openings or, simply, the Oaks. Not nearly enough trees to call it a forest, way too many to call it a prairie. Biologists call it oak savanna.

To label the area an oak savanna, though, is too restrictive. It is also wet prairie, sand barrens and wet woods crammed into a natural area that covers only 130 square miles. Even with changes wrought by civilization, over 1,000 plant species thrive here, including Ohio's largest concentration of state-listed threatened and endangered species. With the diverse plant life comes an equally rich variety of fauna, including winged insects like butterflies, moths, wasps and dragonflies, many of them rare.

The Oaks is a study in contrasts: a land parched dry yet perpetually moist, both acid and alkaline, open sand and green-canopied savanna. So many habitats in such a small area nurturing an astounding variety of species, some of them found nowhere else in the state. Incredibly, nearly one in every five plant species found in the Oaks (178 at last count) is listed as endangered or threatened in Ohio.

Preceding page: Draining water from the land and controlling natural fires have fostered dense stands of sassafras trees.

Left: Salamanders find the Oak Openings prime habitat.

Right: White oak tree, Glen Helen Nature Preserve, Greene County.

Early settlers didn't care what it was called, for them it was simply welcome relief. Just to the east was the Great Black Swamp, a huge morass that was known as the most desolate wilderness in America. West-bound pioneer wagons crawled through the mire of the Great Black Swamp, sometimes traveling only a mile a day. They emerged from the swamp into the Oak Openings where they could follow high dry sand ridges, easily steering their teams and wagons through the openings.

They neither knew nor cared that the sand beneath their wagons was ancient beach sand, sand deposited by a much larger post-glacial predecessor to Lake Erie called Lake Warren. When Warren retreated, it left its western beaches and sand bars high and dry, sand that became the foundation for the Oak Openings.

Wind relentlessly sculpted the sand, piling it fifty feet deep and more in some places. The resulting undulating landscape is one of dunes and swales. On the dunes, high above the water table, only the hardy sun-loving plants survive, plants with expansive root systems able to tap deep into the dunes for life-giving moisture. Oak trees and plants of the tallgrass prairie thrive here.

Between the dunes, in the low areas where the water table is at or near the surface, are stands of swamp forest and wet prairie. Natural drainage is very poor in the Oaks and before the coming of man-made ditches, water often stood between the dunes for much of the year.

Stories abound about orchids so numerous that farmers once brought them to market by the wagonload, and about wet prairies so extensive that Native Americans could canoe uninterrupted for several miles at a stretch through stands of sedges and wild rice which nurtured huge flocks of waterfowl.

Preceding page: A few thousand years ago a trip to these high and dry sand dunes would have been a day at the beach. It is this sand that defines the Oak Openings, deep layers of sand blown into an undulating landscape.

Right: Right: Gentians and Sumac, Oak Openings Preserve.

From the Edge

Fire is a controlling force in the Oak Openings. With it the prairie plants thrive, without it saplings and cool weather grasses invade and overtake the plants of the tallgrass prairie.

But it is not a conflagration, an explosive wall of fire racing across the prairie. Quite the opposite. The low flames creep slowly and evenly across the floor of the oak savanna sending smoke billowing into the spreading crowns of the scattered treetops.

It often happens in the early spring when the savanna floor is piled deep in oak leaves dried by the brisk winds of the season. The wind pushes the flames through the leaves, boiling the rising sap in seedlings and killing shallow rooted plants.

In the wake of the fire, the spring sun reaches the savanna floor through still-leafless branches, warming the blackened soil, giving the prairie plants an early boost. Within weeks the rich green leaves of prairie dock and the lavender blooms of lupine, a plant the rarest of Oak Openings butterflies rely on, will emerge. Persius dusky wing, frosted elfin and the federally endangered Karner Blue butterfly count on lupine as the food plant for their larva. Lupine is making a comeback in the Oaks but apparently not quickly enough for the Karner Blue—the last one was seen in 1989.

Left: Fire is the blood of the Oak Openings, releasing nutrients and giving the warm-season prairie species the growth advantage over the common cool-weather plants. When applied under very controlled conditions, fire is a beneficial and integral part of the Oak Openings ecology.

Right: Karner Blue butterfly on lupine flower stalk.

In the middle of the open dunes, close to Ohio's best patch of sand cherry, a pair of lark sparrows are raising a brood of four. If successful, they'll help swell Ohio's population beyond the twelve known nesting pairs, all of them in the Oaks. They forage for insects among the sprouting stands of blazing star, western sunflower and a host of other rare plants.

Foraging, too, are the bluebirds, the bird that wears the sky on its back. Still working to feed their first brood, they'll nest once, maybe twice more before the end of summer. They're not the only ones searching for insects. A variety of flycatchers, warblers and sparrows join the feast.

In the wet areas the real magic begins when the orchids bloom in late spring. Yellow lady's-slippers, grass pinks, purple and orange fringed orchids add elegant color. With summer, butterfly weed is at its best, serving up nectar to countless of its namesakes.

In the cooler edges of the sand, slithering marks reveal the passing of more than one kind of snake. One, perhaps a hognose, has simply passed through. The second, a large female blue racer, has laid her eggs in a sandy bank. If the racer is the long sleek sports car of reptiles, the hognose is the practical utility vehicle. The racer will hold its head high and speed across openings and through cover. The hognose is slow and stout, but it has a bag of tricks that include flattening its head like a cobra, attempting to frighten its would-be predator with mock strikes. If that doesn't work it will go limp and play dead.

Spending June on the wooded edges of the high dry sand dunes suits the snakes just fine. Better still that the savanna and dunes are only yards away from wet areas where amphibians breed explosively in rain-swollen pools. Wood frogs, spring peepers, chorus frogs and a healthy variety of salamanders are among the species that begin life there.

Three sets of tiny deer tracks among a larger set mark the passing of a doe and triplet fawns across the dunes. Raccoon and fox tracks are thick along the edges. Tiny and not so tiny holes in the sand reveal the presence of a variety of sand wasps, bigger burrows accommodate a colony of cicada killers which feast on the abundant cicadas signaling the heart of summer with the din of their rattling call.

The heart of summer soon fades, replaced by the brilliant colors of fall. It is a relentless cycle that will soon bring winter's cold and, finally, a return to spring.

The Oak Openings, like every natural area, is magical in any season. Each day, each hour, is special in its own way.

GLACIAL
RELICS
BOG & FEN

*I*ce Age Ohio conjures images of a bitterly cold, desolate landscape locked in perpetual winter.

Some 20,000 years ago the last glacier—geologists call it the Wisconsinan glacier—made its farthest advances into Ohio, covering nearly all of the western part of the state and a third of the eastern part. In the north, along present-day Lake Erie, the ice was an incredible mile and a half thick, high enough that just the increase in surface elevation created a climate in which snow fell throughout the year.

But along the leading edge of the glacier, which was only 50 to 100 feet thick, the climate was much friendlier. Though an overall 10 to 20 degrees cooler than today's average temperatures, the land saw the passing of all four seasons. Forests grew and flowers bloomed in the summer shadows of the icy wall.

Preceding page: Frame Lake, Portage County/Herrick Fen State Nature Preserve.

Left: Roundleaf sundew catches a cricket meal.

Right: The glacial grooves on Kelley's Island in Lake Erie are among the most accessible and well-known in the world. These dramatic footprints of the glacier, ground into limestone, measure 400 feet long, 30 feet wide, and 15 feet deep.

Of course the species that flourished weren't the warm-weather plants Ohioans are most familiar with. The trees and wildflowers were typical of the northern forests of Canada. Spruce, fir, pine, hemlock and tamarack—trees with needles instead of leaves—dominated. As the climate warmed, the glacier receded and the needle trees crept northward, claiming the land as quickly as the glacier relinquished it.

Hard on the heels of the needle trees came the oaks, maples and beeches of the deciduous forest. Better adapted to the climbing temperatures, the warm-weather broadleaf forest eventually pushed the once-dominant needle forest from Ohio.

The needle trees didn't disappear from Ohio, though, nor did many of the other northern ferns and wildflowers. Many of them are rare now, found in only a handful of special places. Somehow they've managed to hang on, here and there, in the nooks and crannies of the face of Ohio.

Some plants have been able to hang on because of the glacier itself. The glacier, nature's earthmover, bulldozed the landscape, smoothing plains and rounding rocky ridges. Like a bulldozer it pushed along soil, gravel and boulders—glacial till—in unbelievable quantities. When the glacier receded it left the till behind. Canada's loss was Ohio's gain.

In places it also left behind huge chunks of ice. Some of these stranded icebergs, buried in the insulating till, took centuries to melt, leaving deep water-filled depressions that today are seen as kettle lakes and bogs.

Left: Stewart Lake, Scioto Trail State Park.

Right: Buttonbush in fall, Charles Dembach Preserve, Geauga County.

Left: Tamarack and understory in fall color, Herrick Fen State Nature Preserve.

Right: Tamarack, a tree of the North Woods, came with the glaciers and stayed, well-suited to the edges of the Ohio bogs. Unlike most conifers, the tamarack is deciduous, its clumps of green needles yellow and drop with autumn. It can hang onto its small cones, though, for years.

Gifts of the Glaciers

In . . . out . . . Who cares which way the water flows? It matters a lot to those in the business of learning about bogs and fens.

Some people call both bogs, some refer to fens as alkaline bogs. No matter the terminology, they are glacial treasures counted among Ohio's most special natural places.

Bogs are basins: water flows in, not out. Sphagnum moss, a prolific plant of the north, took an early hold in the stagnant post-glacial waters, helping turn bog waters highly acidic. Sphagnum grows in floating mats, extending and, in some cases, completely covering the deep open waters. The mats intertwine and grow both in breadth and depth until sometimes they're thick enough and strong enough to support the weight of large mammals or even mature trees. Even me.

On Shaky Ground

It felt more than a little like I was walking on a water bed. The northeast Ohio ground beneath my feet wasn't ground at all, but a floating sphagnum mat that over centuries gained thickness and strength until it could support even white pines.

Though the day was sunny and hot, the air above the mat was cool and humid, testimony to the mat's ability to wick and hold large quantities of water from the deep, cool waters of the kettle lake below. The mat itself, by acting as an insulating blanket, helped keep the lake's water cool.

I had walked through an upland oak woods to reach the bog, then through a mixed hardwood and pine forest and was now passing through a stand of mature white pines that thinned the closer I came to the edge of the mat and the open waters of the lake. The stand frequently opened onto gaping clearings where a large pine had toppled to earth, its broad but shallow root ball torn and standing upright. Where it once stood was a shallow water-filled hole, testimony to lurking lake waters.

It was like walking to the center of a target. Concentric circles of different kinds of vegetation emanated from the open water bull's-eye. The closer to the bull's eye, the shorter the vegetation, the less shade, the harsher the environment.

In from the pines were shrubs: winterberry, leatherleaf, poison sumac and the like. Then the open seedbed, home to sedges and rushes, the rare calopogon or grass-pink orchid and the insect-eating sundews and pitcher plants.

Ahead, where the mat was not stable enough for walking, it was only sphagnum on water. From oak forest to water the distance was only a few hundred yards. But in that distance I had traveled, in plant terms, from Ohio's oak forest to the Arctic Circle.

Spring-fed stream (note ridge surrounding fen) in Gallagher Fen State Nature Preserve.

Repeat After Me, "Bog, In. Fen, Out"

Water flows into a bog, out from a fen. Bogs are highly acidic, fens are highly alkaline. Both represent harsh environments where only the most well-adapted plants can survive. Sounds simple, but people get them mixed up all the time. Even names don't always help. The highly celebrated Cedar Bog near Urbana is really a fen.

Like their bog relatives, fens are products of the glaciers. Both are water-cooled environments: bogs by the cold lake or pond waters beneath the sphagnum mat, fens generally by cold springs which gurgle forth from limestone-rich formations of glacial till. While bog waters stagnate, fens are constantly flushed.

Bull's-eye for a fen is the spring where the cold water gurgles forth oxygen-poor but rich in calcium and magnesium. Life is tough at the bull's-eye, an area often called the marl meadow, where the white of lime deposits can sometimes be seen on the soil. A few sedges are joined by such unusual plants as calopogon, bunchflower, fringed gentian and, in some fens, the insect-eaters, sundew and pitcher plant.

Farther away from the spring is the fen meadows, an area of taller, thicker growing plants. In drier portions of the fen meadow are plants of the tallgrass prairie including Indian grass, prairie dock and blazing star.

Bogs and, especially, fens, were never common in Ohio and, until the appearance of another glacier, there won't be any more than there are today.

Nature has joined humans in a conspiracy threatening the demise of those that exist.

Periodic drought steals the water the rare bog and fen plants rely on. The forest and shrubs that surround them apply constant pressure to move in, slowly but surely drawing their circle tighter. Nature works to fill these low spots with silt, leaves and other plant materials. Humans have done their own share of filling and draining for agriculture, of mining the gravel for construction and developing the sites for housing.

Ohio's bogs and fens are rare jewels, to be appreciated not only for their obvious beauty but for the treasures they hold. Beneath the surface of beautiful plants and wildflowers, buried in the layers of sphagnum, is information. Information that scientists can use as keys to unlock the past, adding to our understanding of the plants that preceded those seen today.

Think of them as nature's prehistory book.

HOCKING
HILLS

*H*ocking Hills wasn't built in a day, a year or even a thousand years.

Water droplets, falling from vegetation, gather briefly on shallow soil then move on as one in a seemingly insignificant trickle to a small brook which tumbles to a small rill. The rill feeds a lazy creek that gurgles to a small river and it to a larger one. Along the way the passing droplets loosen and break away minute amounts of sand particles from the sandstone bedrock.

In winter, mere ounces of water gather in tiny fissures and freeze, the force of the expanding water imperceptibly widening the fissures. In spring the ice thaws and flows to the brook to the creek to the river, joining torrents of thawwaters in swollen streams.

Measured in human lifetimes the impact of billions of water droplets is seemingly insignificant. To the casual human eye the stream channels flow no deeper, the cliff face is no more worn than a century before. Here and there a slump block might have sheered off a cliff. Otherwise, things would seem status quo.

Multiply these minute changes over the length of a million human lifetimes, though, and the results are dramatic.

Much of Ohio counts back a few tens of thousands of years, back to the last of the great glaciers, to measure the origins of its surface features. But most of Hocking Hills looks back 350 million years when the sands that were to become the famous Blackhand Sandstone were deposited as deltas by streams and rivers that rushed from alp-like mountains to a sea that covered much of Ohio.

When the great sea disappeared, the land rose and the ancient pre-glacial Teays River system began carving its magic in a palette of 250-foot-deep sandstone deposits.

Preceding page: Leaning pine trees, at cliff's edge, Conkles Hollow State Nature Preserve.

Inset: An American woodcock is well camouflaged in its surroundings.

Right: Blue Hen Falls, Cuyahoga Valley National Recreation Area.

From a Mere Drop

It was a light rain, a very gentle rain, adding a sheen to the greenery of late spring that hung everywhere in the hollows of Hocking Hills. A rain that added an almost imperceptible amount of water to the nameless stream that created Conkles Hollow.

There, on the east rim of Conkles Hollow, on the single most breathtaking spot in the most beautiful public site in arguably the most beautiful area of Ohio, the story of Hocking Hills begins to unfold. It is a chapter written by "The Little Stream That Could"—a chapter that is a monument to persistence.

The Little Stream That Could is so obscure it carries no name. It runs but a short distance from just above Conkles, through the gorge and on to Pine Creek at the hollow's mouth. Most of the year it's only a few inches deep and is narrow enough to be jumped across. Yet its handiwork is undeniable.

Over the millennia, the stream has slashed a channel over 200 feet deep into the Blackhand Sandstone, creating a hollow over a half-mile long, twice as high as it is wide and guarded over its entire length by spectacular, sheer cliffs. It is, by most accounts, the deepest gorge in Ohio.

It is a world unto itself, full of waterfalls and caves. The deep recesses of the gorge are cool and damp, harboring healthy populations of giant hemlock trees, Canada yew, teaberry, partridgeberry and other more northern species marooned after the glacier retreated. At the northern-facing mouth of the hollow, where the Little Stream That Could meets Pine Creek is one of the best stands of river birch in Ohio.

Preceding page: Conkles
Hollow State Nature Preserve.

Left: Cedar Falls, Hocking
Hills State Park.

To a Multitude of Wonders

In stark contrast to the cool, rich soils of the cliff-shaded valley are the brutally dry, shallow soils of the sunny ridgetops supporting sparse stands of oak and pine, blueberries, huckleberries and mountain laurel.

Black bear, mountain lion, elk and marten once roamed the area. Beaver, whitetail deer, grouse, turkey and bobcat still do. The species are fascinating but it is the view that astounds. It is the view from the gorge floor looking up at towering cross-bedded and honeycombed cliffs or from the Hollow's rim across a river of trees banked by the grays and pastels of the rocky ramparts spilling into the Pine Creek valley. There is an aura of wildness, of untamed nature, of rugged survival.

The aura intensifies on a crisp fall morning, when fog hangs thick and full in the cool gorge until the sun's warmth boils it away in steam-like wisps.

At such times, there is an urge to return in another hundred thousand years or so and see what new magic the Little Stream That Could has worked.

For the present, we have the inspiring wonders of Conkles, Old Man's Cave, Cedar Falls, Airplane Rock, Cantwell Cliffs, Ash Cave and Rock House.

The shape of the Old Man's Cave gorge suggests how this region got its name. Hocking is from the native name for the main river of the region, "Hockhocking," which means bottle river. The bottle is from the shape of the gorges, narrower at the top, wider at the gorge floor.

Left: Rock House is the most
unusual of Ohio's recess
caves, sporting seven
"windows" in a cliff of
Blackhand sandstone opening
into rooms that connect in a
house of rock.

Above: Black bear once
roamed the Hocking Hills and,
perhaps, someday will again.
Gone from Ohio for years,
there are now a handful of
black bears known to have
migrated into the state from
neighboring Pennsylvania and
West Virginia where black
bears thrive.

HILL
COUNTRY

Geologists call it the unglaciated Appalachian Plateau, others call it part of the Appalachian Highlands, but most people refer to it as, simply, Hill Country. Covering the southeastern third of the state, Hill Country, as its name suggests, is no longer the unmarred plateau it was when it rose from an ancient sea millions of years ago.

Maturely dissected is the formal term to describe the condition of today's plateau. Rugged works just as well. Water and wind have conspired over millions of years to created a labyrinth of hills and hollows.

This is the tree-whiskered craggy face of Ohio, the only part of the state that didn't get a glacial face-lift. Though untouched by the glaciers it wasn't unaffected. Torrents of meltwater flowing away from the retreating glacier cut deep into layers of sandstone, shale and limestone.

Trees established footholds everywhere there was soil to grab, making this area an incredible expanse of unbroken virgin forest virtually devoid of natural openings. Even today, except where the landscape is opened for homes, industry or farming, the Southeast is heavily forested. Many of those wounds are healing as reclaimed strip mines and farms which failed in the poor, shallow hillside soils slowly revert to woodland.

Preceding page: Golden evening under cirrus clouds near Logan, Hocking County.

Left: Young opossum on a branch.

Right: Cedar Falls, Hocking Hills State Park.

White, red and scarlet oaks join hickory in dominating the ridgetops. Mixed mesophytic forests—a forest in which a large number of trees share dominance—cover, especially, north-facing slopes. Tulip trees, beeches, sugar maples and ash are among the roughly two dozen species of trees of the mixed forest. Deep in the rich soil of the ravines are hemlock, sycamore, elm. A variety of pines, many of them planted for harvest because they do well in dry, poor soils, also thrive here.

Not surprisingly, it is Hill Country that supports the greatest acreages of state parks, forests and natural areas, as well as the Wayne National Forest. Mohican, Salt Fork, Burr Oak, Lake Hope, Hocking Hills and Shawnee State Parks are all popular travel destinations. Shawnee State Forest and Park, some 62,000 acres of nearly unbroken forest, is the largest contiguous forest in the state.

Preceding page: Autumn abstract.

Pine Forest, Mitchell Forest, Hamilton County.

Left: Golden ragwart on vernal stream, Shawnee State Forest.

Right: Pheasant on courtship log.

The Nurturing Hills

Listen, listen, listen. Concentrate, so hard that your ears start to hum.

Listen through the first light of dawn for the tell-tale sound of a male wild turkey summoning its hens. But the only sound that echos from ridge to ridge, across the hollows of part of the Wayne National Forest east of Marietta, is the distinctive "Who cooks for you, who cooks for you all," call of the barred owl.

Not so long ago it would have been futile to even try listening for a gobbler. Once present throughout Ohio, the bird that very nearly became our national symbol was gone, their numbers decimated by habitat loss and diseases spread by domestic poultry.

The Ohio Division of Wildlife began reintroduction efforts in the mid-1950s and today the wild turkey is back in more than half of Ohio's eighty-eight counties. Their ideal habitat is the mature deciduous forest with scattered clearings where they can forage for their complex diet of seeds, acorns, fruits and grasses. With its isolated nooks and crannies, Hill Country was the perfect place to nurture its comeback.

From one of those crannies a distant rattle breaks the silence, a gobbler rising to challenge the barred owl's call. Then another gobbler and, after a time, yet another. It is Hill Country's call of the wild, a call that sends a shiver of satisfaction down the back. A symbol of all the good things happening in Ohio's wilds.

It speaks for the eagle, bobcat and heron, all of which have found secure Ohio homes. It speaks for the big whitetail buck that explodes from the edge of a swamp, nostrils flared and snorting steam.

Left: White-tailed doe in early morning.

Right: It is the gobbler, not the rooster, that Ohioans now yearn to hear with the dawn. A wild symbol of the successful return of many species to the Buckeye state, the wild turkey has reestablished its range over much of Ohio.

Virtually extinct in Ohio at the turn of the century, whitetail deer had gone the way of mountain lions, bisons and bears. Massive deforestation for logging and agriculture, coupled with unrestricted hunting, caused the whitetail's near demise. But they hung on, their population, like the turkey's, was nurtured back to healthy numbers. And as Hill Country recovered, so did the whitetail. Today's herd is huge, too huge perhaps, achieving greater numbers than there were two hundred years ago.

Less numerous but with just as much presence is nature's lumberjack, the beaver. It was also gone from Ohio but has made a dramatic recovery, sometimes to the frustration of county highway engineers who find the industrious animal flooding a roadway.

Nurtured, too, is a whole host of plants and animals, wondrous species both familiar and virtually unknown.

Right: Snake Hollow stream, Shawnee State Forest.

Inset: Beaver at streamside for a midday drink.

Deep in Hill Country's Jackson County, about as far south as you can go without splashing in the Ohio River, is the 1,800 acre Lake Katherine State Nature Preserve, one of the most biologically diverse areas in the state. Deep in a precipitously walled hemlock gorge, across a beautiful woodland stream, is a stand of tall spindly trees, out of place in an Ohio forest.

Bigleaf magnolias, they're called, one of four species of magnolia found in Ohio and by far the rarest. Only a few thousand of the trees survive at Lake Katherine, one of only three places in Ohio where they grow. Only forty or so grow in just the right conditions to reach maturity, to flower and produce seeds.

It's most commonly found in Mississippi and Alabama, but even there it's generally scarce. Jackson County, Ohio, is as far north as the tree is found, most likely arriving there courtesy of the pre-glacial Teays River system. The bigleafs, like so many other Ohio treasures, take their nurturing in Hill Country's nooks, hanging on in only a few deep, rocky, protected sandstone gorges where they find stable habitat, moisture and protection from the extremes of wind and temperature.

Up the walls of the gorges, gently swaying in the sunshine of June, the spindly magnolias show off. Thirty feet up, shaded among the protective flapping of three-foot-long and one-foot-wide leaves, are its flowers. Large and showy, they sport eight-inch-long petals.

As the big leaves flap, so do the wings of a nearby ruffed grouse. Somewhere, perhaps a quarter mile away or more, a male grouse stands on its log, cups his wings and with each flap sends a low-pitched drumming sound through the woodland. It is a signal to other males that the territory is taken.

No matter, there are plenty of other places in the nurturing nooks of Hill Country.

Left: The drumming of grouse is a common sound in Hill Country.

Right: Nature's artistry is displayed in autumn colors.

The Great Forest

$\mathcal{T}$ake one part rich soil, one part sand, one part abundant water supply and one part favorable climate. Mix well and apply in a variety of combinations across Ohio and no self-respecting tree can resist the temptation to put down its roots.

Oh my, how they put down roots. A vast, though not unbroken, hardwood forest dominated Ohio, perhaps the richest hardwood forest ever to grace the earth. It wasn't just the expanse of forest that impressed, it was the mixture and the unbelievable size of individual trees.

Preceding page: Cuyahoga National Recreation Area.

Left: Shagbark hickory in Dysart Woods.

Inset: Dutchman's Breeches, Fowler Woods State Nature Peserve.

Right: Marsh marigolds in Fowler Woods.

Location, location, location

Perhaps nowhere is the fate of Ohio's primeval forests more dramatically illustrated than northwest Ohio's Great Black Swamp. This huge swamp's woods stretched unbroken along Lake Erie from Port Clinton all the way to the Maumee River.

The mire of water, muck and trees proved to be formidable to settlers, both historic and prehistoric. Its mere presence delayed development of northwest Ohio nearly one hundred years behind the rest of the state.

The swamp forest was extremely rich and many of the trees were huge. Some early pioneers wrote that upon approaching the Black Swamp it loomed in the distance as a great blue wall, a perpetual haze created by the transpiration of so many huge trees.

Piece by piece, tract by tract, the first settlers, then builders and developers whittled away at the once impregnable swamp. The first scars were minor. Pioneer lumbermen invaded the forest and stole away with its choicest trees—black walnut for gun stocks, black cherry for furniture, huge oaks for the New England clipper ships. Then came more aggressive lumbering and then, only a century or so ago, clearcutting and draining the land for agriculture.

Today, except for a few precious parcels, all trace of the swamp is gone. In its place is a flat, open landscape blessed with a rich, black topsoil supporting row after row of corn and soybeans. Only untold miles of deep drainage ditches betray the land's waterlogged ancestry.

So it is through much of Ohio's farm country, where the land was cleared for agriculture. Many of Ohio's giants were simply girdled, felled and burned, turning untold numbers of logs of superior hardwood into ash piles. The farmland that replaced the forest was rich, but the ecological loss was staggering.

"The" tree in Dysart Woods is a tulip tree which rises straight as an arrow above the forest canopy. Ohio is blessed with a number of huge specimens preserved in the remnants of the great forest.

In southeast Ohio the great forest didn't fall so much to open the land for agriculture as for timber, mining and iron ore production. In the Hanging Rock Iron Region, which in the 1800s satisfied much of the nation's iron needs, acre after acre of virgin timber fell to woodcutters frantically trying to keep the furnaces supplied with charcoal to fuel their hearths.

It's debatable how many truly virgin stands of woodland remain in Ohio, for the woodsman's ax penetrated nearly every woods to at least remove choice specimens. But many old woodlands dot the state: oak-hickory woods, beech-maple forests and ancient specimens of hemlock and white cedar hidden in hollows and gorges. They survived in places like Fowler Woods State Nature Preserve because of benevolent landowners. Others survived as farmers' woodlots, often in sections too low and swampy to be drained for farming. Still others escaped because of remote locations too deep in a gorge or too far up a hollow to be worth the work of cutting and hauling.

The magnificence and diversity of Ohio's big woods survives in places like Goll Woods, Johnson Woods, Hach-Otis State Nature Preserves, Hueston Woods National Natural Landmark and Dysart Woods.

Tall Timber

On the map it's marked simply, "Tulip Tree."

Four hundred fifty-five acres in all, some fifty acres of Dysart Woods in Belmont County is labeled primeval oak forest, the largest known remnant of the original forest of southeastern Ohio. Some of the oaks are over three hundred years old, measuring 4 feet in diameter and 140 feet in height.

Even so, the only tree marked on the Dysart Woods map is the tulip tree. You can get to it by cutting diagonally down a steep slope past a hillside of large beech trees, then down farther through a forest of great oaks and hickories. Cross the stream, take a left and you'll be standing breathless, looking at one of the biggest trees to be seen anywhere.

Two hundred years ago a tree of that magnitude might not have warranted more than a cursory glance. It would have been just another big tree in a vast forest of big trees. But today it and its neighbors are goliaths in a world that judges large and small by substantially different standards than the world of the pioneers.

More than half a football field tall, seventeen feet in girth, from its considerable foundation it shoots straight as an arrow through the forest canopy. The grayish thin bark it sported during its youth when Ohio wasn't yet Ohio, has browned and deeply furrowed with age.

A tree of this sort can't be appreciated from a distance. Intimacy is requisite. Stroke the bark to feel its age. Lean against it, hug it to feel its strength and size. Stand at its base and crane the neck to appreciate its reach for the heavens, its domination over all else in the forest.

Tulip Tree (right) and maple tree glow in springtime sun, Conckles Hollow State Nature Preserve.

Following page: Filtered light silhouettes a deer at sunrise.

Nature's High-Rise Dwellings

Looking down from such heights with an equally impressive view, are the creatures of the tall timber. Nomadic raccoons find precipitous sleeping quarters on the open crotches and in hollows. Woodpeckers, creepers and nuthatches scour the tall shanks cleansing the tree of insects attacking its bark defense. Tanagers and other birds of the treetops are common, though thought to be uncommon simply because they live their lives, out of sight, in the canopy. Northern flying squirrels, also much more common than thought, live in the excavations of woodpeckers, exiting after sunset for their nocturnal swoops.

Perhaps a barred owl will stare down with its innocent, liquid black eyes. More likely it will be the angry yellow eyes of the master of Ohio's woods, the great horned owl.

The beautiful, though savage, great horned owl may owe its nasty disposition to its role as Ohio's earliest nesting bird. In the dead of winter, when the mercury has bottomed out and snow fills the skies, before the calendar even flips to February, the female great horned owl is shivering on her clutch of two, maybe three, eggs.

Winter doesn't set them back, their keen sense of directional hearing enables them to detect prey moving beneath the snow. Sometimes they store their prey, defrosting it later by "incubating" it. Rodents are high on their favored food list along with rabbits and some birds. Unfortunately, "some birds" includes any of Ohio's other species of owls they can get their talons on.

Today the great horned is found throughout Ohio. But it wasn't always so. It was thought to be very rare at the time of settlement. But because it's a species able to survive in a variety of habitats, it's been able to flourish while other owls are on the decline.

Sunlight punctures the canopy of Miami-Whitewater Forest in Hamilton County. On the shaded forest floor, wildflowers must hurry to bloom in spring before the trees leaf out and cut off their sun.

King of the Woods

The great horned owl may be the most common resident of the woodland darkness but it is the pileated woodpecker that some have dubbed "king-of-the-woods."

Better to call it the jackhammer of the big woods, or stump breaker. The logcock, as it is also called, is by far the largest of Ohio's woodpeckers, yet is so secretive it is seldom seen. Its presence, though, is betrayed by its loud ringing call, its rhythmical drumming and its unmistakable handiwork.

In pursuit of ants infesting a tree, it will hammer away with precise blows, its big bill chiseling away chips like a woodcutter, stopping only to sample the insects it has exposed. Often, its more or less rectangular excavations will extend down to the heartwood, eight inches or more in height, four inches or more in width.

It is the heavy-duty contractor of the trees, inadvertently filling an important role as maker of homes for all kinds of tree-dwelling animals that can't excavate their own.

The pileated-built homes overlook an undisturbed forest floor that in spring is covered with colorful masses of trillium, spring-beauty, marsh marigold, Dutchman's-breeches and trout lily.

It's one of nature's greatest shows in a cathedral of ancient trees.

Left: White-flowered trillium.

Inset: The pileated woodpecker not only favors the mature forests of Ohio but research suggests stands older than a half century are necessary for nesting territories.

Right: Bluebells, Cedar Fork Gorge National Area, Ashland County.

PASSAGES
OF LIFE
RIVERS
& STREAMS

ater is Ohio's lifeblood. Groundwater, springs, lakes, streams, marshes and swamps, bogs and fens—they nurture plants, spawn new life, harbor popular game fish like muskellunge and walleye as well as the obscure, like the knobbed rock shell and rabbit's foot mussels.

Thousands of miles of waterways, square miles of lakes and ponds, big and small, named and unnamed. Billions upon billions of gallons of freshwater without even counting the treasure held in massive underground aquifers. It is a gift that keeps on giving—every Ohio region averages at least thirty inches of precipitation each year, many are drenched with forty or even more.

Ohio streams are more than just nature's watery highways, they are the ties that bind. Bounded sometimes by walls of rock, sometimes by broad floodplains made rich by the deposits of spring floods, they are ribbons of life that flow obliviously, though generally not unaffected, past industry and homes.

Their open waters, shielded by wooded banks, are migration corridors, providing safe passage, food and shelter for huge numbers of migrating songbirds and waterfowl.

And they are places of great beauty sporting great names. The Maumee, Muskingum, Vermilion, Scioto, Little Beaver, Little Miami, Stillwater, the Clear Fork of the Mohican, Chagrin and the Grand are among them.

Preceding page: Plentiful
water blesses much of Ohio,
creating beauty where it
courses in streams.

Right: Autumn overlook at
Tinkers Creek National
Natural Landmark.

Renewed Presence

The river otter had gone the way of the panther, wolf, bison and bear. Overharvested for its rich pelt, intolerant of the changes that settlement brought to the pristine waters of its home ranges, this long-bodied, short-legged member of the weasel family disappeared.

Now it is back. In northeast Ohio, in the shadow of Cleveland, along the wild upper reaches of the Grand River, the otter has found a home. Secured from Louisiana in a swap of wild turkey for river otter, the Ohio Division of Wildlife has brought the playful otter back to Ohio.

Glacial slumps are what they call the sometimes steep valley walls of the Grand River. Composed of clay and sand, the walls are perfect raw materials for otters to throw their large weasel-like bodies down, sliding to the river. Though it may be for sheer play, the slides also represent a quicker way to travel than on stumpy legs.

Though not clumsy on land, the otter is built for aquatic travel, swimming underwater, chasing down prey of fish and frogs and other denizens of the streams, all of them relying on clean water for survival.

Morning fog over the Ohio River valley.

Flexing Mussels

A good indication of clean water is a healthy mussel population in a stream. Mussels feed by drawing water inside their shells, filtering out the tiny organisms they feed on and driving the water out of their shells. Silt clogs the mechanism, chemical pollution kills, so the presence of a healthy variety of mussels means the water is clean.

The Big and Little Darby Creeks west of Columbus and the Ohio Brush Creek between Cincinnati and Portsmouth sit high on the list of mussel streams. At least forty species of mussels can be found in the Darby system, more than two dozen in Ohio Brush Creek, including many rare species in each. Their names have character—yellow sandshell, pocket book, pistol grip, painted elktoe and northern riffleshell—but not enough character to overcome the difficulty of raising public concern. It's relatively easy to excite people about saving Ohio's bald eagles, but a mussel rally wouldn't attract much attention.

Still, mussels are important examples of something worth protecting. They survive in streams where there is little shoreline development, where there is a healthy natural buffer along their lengths, where development has been responsibly balanced with preservation.

Where they survive, so do healthy populations of fish, mammals and birds.

Preceding page: Greenville Creek, one of Ohio's designated scenic rivers, along with nearby Still River, near Covington spreads itself in riffles over shallow ledges in preparation for cascading another 28 feet at Greenville Falls State Nature Preserve.

Left: An interesting sight, river otters on land.

Right: Mussels are prime indicators of stream quality. Clean, silt-free streams are prerequisite for their presence.

The Incredible
Reversing River

It's been estimated that the gently gurgling waters of the Clear Fork of the Mohican River once gushed in a torrent one hundred times as large as it does today. The torrent, an enraged reaction to a glacially dictated change of flow, cut the deep, narrow Clear Fork Gorge.

The gorge cuts through a high plateau that was a divide between two watersheds. With the last glacier, the flow of the northern watershed was blocked by the advancing wall of ice, pooling the waters into a lake that deepened until it spilled over the divide, its waters rushing into the other watershed. Glacial meltwaters swelled the stream, their force cutting the V-shaped gorge through sandstone and shale. The narrowest section of the gorge marks the divide.

Most streams find their source among deep gorges and high ridges, resting downstream in flatter, more open plains. Not so the Mohican. It flows from gentle country into the rugged. Nowhere is it more impressive than at the Clearfork Gorge. A thousand feet wide and three hundred feet deep, it is a National Natural Landmark that shelters stands of towering hemlock and virgin white pine. Fifteen species of warblers nestle within its protective walls, including the northern parula, cerulean and hooded warblers.

Mohican River at dawn, Mohican State Park.

Little Beaver Creek is so far east in Ohio that even the towns have a foreign flavor—East Liverpool, Lisbon, East Palestine and Calcutta. Throw a rock and just about hit the Ohio River, Pennsylvania or West Virginia.

Little Beaver Creek was designated as the state's first wild and scenic river in 1974. Shortly thereafter it gained the distinction as Ohio's first national scenic river.

Most people meet this wild stream at Beaver Creek State Park where it has cut a deep valley through the rolling forested foothills of the Alleghenies. But the entire valley is beautiful, including large tracts of privately held lands still in their natural state.

It is the flagship of Ohio's officially designated scenic and wild rivers, a list that now includes ten rivers totaling nearly 650 miles. In addition to the Little Beaver and the Little Miami, which makes its most beautiful mark in Clifton Gorge, the Big and Little Darby Creeks also have national stature.

Left: Trout lilies grow in profusion in the floodplain of the Vermilion River, a section preserved by the Ohio Division of Natural Areas and Preserves.

Right: Little Beaver Creek, known for its beautiful overlooks, was Ohio's first designated wild river in 1974, and the state's second national scenic river the following year.

OPEN COUNTRY
PRAIRIES, DUNES & MEADOWS

*O*pen spaces aren't empty spaces.

It's a difficult concept. Trees are easy to understand. They're good, they have value, Smokey the Bear said so. Trees fill a landscape, block the view, make their presence obvious.

Nature's open spaces—meadows, prairies, dunes and wetlands—fill a landscape, too, but in a very different way. Open and treeless translates into a land of opportunity for a host of plants and wildlife that can't compete in the shadow of the forest. Far from being empty spaces, open spaces are teeming with life and opportunities for discovery.

Preceding page: Ohio's best lakeshore dunes are in Headlands Dunes State Nature Preserve near Mentor.

Left: Beach pea is typical of the standard Atlantic coastal species to be found in Headlands Dunes, remnants of a time when an ancient sea stretched inland to Ohio.

Right: Dunes are among the most changeable of Ohio's natural environments. These transient sand patterns are at Conneaut Harbor.

At the Beach

Is it Cape Cod? Anyone who's been to Cape Cod would see the similarities. The waves that break on the beach are clear and blue. The sand is clean, white and covered with beach grasses as it slopes from a tree line, across a sandy swale, then rises to a barrier dune before falling again to the lakeshore beach. American beach grass, little bluestem and switchgrass are the bronco riders of the dunes, trapping the sand, holding on, riding the dunes as they move and change.

Only it's not Cape Cod, it's Headland Dunes State Nature Preserve at Fairport Harbor, east of Cleveland. The clear waters aren't the Atlantic Ocean but Lake Erie lapping onto a mere sixteen acres tucked at the end of a mile-long stretch of sugar-like sand that's been beaten into submission by millions of swimmers' feet.

Still, the small dunes prove the resiliency of nature's open spaces. Not so long ago, Headlands Dunes stood barren and white like the rest of the beach. A simple wooden snow fence was installed, keeping the crush of summer swimmers at bay, slowing the wind-blown sand, trapping it and beginning to build the dunes. Colonizing grasses moved in, helping stabilize and add to the dunes, reestablishing a rare habitat.

Ohio's dunes occurred largely at the western mouths of rivers, the result of river currents interrupting the cross-current of the lake and causing sand deposition. But because Lake Erie is sand-poor compared to the other Great Lakes, dunes are less common in Ohio.

Mixed among the dune grasses is a variety of Atlantic Coastal species such as sea rocket, beach pea and seaside spurge, species that can't be found growing any farther inland than Ohio. Credit the glaciers with their presence. Constant movement of water between the coast and the retreating edge of the glacier in Ohio enabled East Coast species to migrate.

Found, too, are xeric plants, plants specially adapted to harsh, dry conditions. Associated with prairies, they made their easternmost extension into Ohio. Little bluestem, winged pigweed and sand dropseed, among others, can be found at Headlands Dunes, where the Atlantic seaboard meets the prairie.

Grasses are the key to Headland Dunes. They are the tough plants that ride the changing dunes, eventually colonizing and stabilizing them. American beach grass is joined by switchgrass, purple sand grass and several prairie grasses in attempting to carpet the dunes in green.

Treeless Plains

Ohio's prairies weren't vast, but they were well established when the European pioneers arrived. The area called the Prairie Peninsula is the finger-like extension of the tallgrass prairies into Ohio. They came complete with a few bison. Many of Ohio's prairies were so-called wet or mesic prairies. Wet or dry, prairies were and are important colonizers in soils that climate and geology have dealt a poor hand.

They're tough, these prairie plants. They can thrive in poor soil, open sun and drought conditions. Some of their leaves are narrow, some are upright, all are adapted to minimize moisture-loss in the face of a withering sun. All are deep-rooted, some eight feet or more, to extract life-giving water from far beneath the surface. To a point, the worse the conditions the more they thrive.

Big bluestem, Indian grass and little bluestem dominate the landscape. Tall coreopsis, blazing-star, coneflower, gentian and prairie-dock are among the flowering plants that show off their purple and yellow blooms in late summer, long after the woodland wildflowers have faded.

They continue to thrive in western Ohio, in relatively small areas that are regularly burned, either by design or by accident. Railroad rights-of-way where passing trains regularly spark fires are prairie strongholds. Resthaven Wildlife Area near Sandusky is an exceptional example of a managed prairie.

Curious that the trains which helped tame the West, help preserve the western plants of Ohio.

Wild lupine, flourishing after a fire in Kitty Todd Preserve, Lucas County.

Wetlands

Open country includes treeless wetlands. And that's an emotional topic, because ninety-five percent of Ohio's wetlands are gone, lost forever.

But it makes what's left all the more precious. Killbuck, Dillon, Killdeer Plains, Mosquito Creek and dozens more—all protectors of prime wetland habitat.

They're still around, everywhere. In pockets around lakes, in bogs and fens, as mudflats along rivers and in marshes, in managed wildlife areas all around the state. And they're rich in wildlife. Herons and sandpipers can be found anywhere in the state. As prime nesting territory in and around the Lake Erie marshes fills, bald eagles are moving inland, setting up territories on inland wetlands and waters. Canada geese have become so common they should be renamed Ohio geese.

Left: A young snowy egret peers down from its nest in a rookery on a Lake Erie Island. The parent herons and egrets make frequent sorties to mainland marshes which they rely on for food. After hatching, the young and adults disperse, occupying Ohio wetlands and river valleys in large numbers.

Right: Fragrant water lily.

The Forgotten Meadow

Pasturelands, meadows and old farmfields reverting to nature are a valuable commodity.

While those concerned with the future welfare of migratory songbirds are sounding the alarm loudest for the preservation of forests to benefit woodland nesting species, in Ohio the most critical issue isn't forests, but fields. The forests are doing quite well. It's the fields that are disappearing.

Not cultivated farmfields, there are plenty of those. It's the fields full of goldenrods and daisies and asters we treasure.

Fields that are the home of dickcissel and meadowlark, bob-o-link and bobwhite quail. Meadows that breed populations of mice and meadow voles for hawks and fox and for barn owls, a species whose precipitous decline is linked to the disappearance of meadows. Bluebirds, too, rely on such areas to forage the insects that make up most of their diet.

Hardly empty space, open country is a whole world unto itself.

Below: A black swallowtail graces the Ohio countryside.

Right: Black-eyed Susans, Cuyahoga Valley National Recreation Area.

ON THE PRECIPICE
ROCK ISLANDS & GORGES

$\mathcal{H}$ere and there, the rocky face of Ohio shows itself.

Beneath the verdant forests and rolling fields, beneath the often rich topsoil, sand, glacial till and the sediment of ancient lakes, is the rocky foundation. Where it does reveal itself, it is in the form of limestone, sandstone, dolomite or shale—all pressurized and fossilized products of ancient seas presented in a neatly layered and stacked geological record of prehistoric Ohio.

Stone quarries and highway cuts have done more than nature to expose rocky Ohio. Even where streams have cut deep into Ohio's surface, they often have to penetrate deep layers of soil and till before finding bedrock bottom.

The places where rocky Ohio shows itself naturally are some of its most valuable jewels. Hocking Hills, Clifton Gorge, Tinkers Creek Gorge, the Lake Erie Islands, the rocky ledges of northeast Ohio, the rocky streams of the Shawnee Hills and next door at Buzzardroost Rock—they represent yet another spectacularly beautiful chapter of wild Ohio.

Preceding page: Dawn breaking through the clouds, Kelly's Island.

Right: Blue Hen Falls, Cuyahoga Valley National Recreation Area.

Heron Heaven

Natural treasure has nothing to do with human comfort. One treasure is a storm-battered pile of rock known as West Sister Island. On a good day—a day with no haze of a summer afternoon—it can be seen, floating in Lake Erie like an apparition, way off Crane Creek State Park or a handful of other nearby places.

Lake Erie fishermen know the island well, it's a landmark for some of the best walleye fishing in the world. More than a few have huddled in its lee to escape Lake Erie's notoriously bad weather. Otherwise, its list of contributions to society is short. Commodore Oliver Hazard Perry put a West Sister dateline on his famous "We have met the enemy and they are ours" message announcing the American capture of a British naval squadron in 1813. It's also been a lighthouse station and served as a target for the military to pummel with shells and bombs.

West Sister is an eighty-two-acre chunk of limestone that's been damaged merchandise ever since the glaciers worked it over more than 10,000 years ago. It is a forbidding and forbidden place. Forbidding because the island's dense trail-less understory is laced with large tree-like specimens of poison ivy and thick stands of stinging nettle. The plants are misery, the insects diabolical.

Human visitors are forbidden anyway on West Sister, Ohio's only federally designated wilderness. As such, it is strictly off limits without explicit permission from the United States Fish and Wildlife Service, which oversees the island as part of the Ottawa National Wildlife Refuge complex.

Welcome and never needing a permit are thousands of herons and other birds that call West Sister home. In its hackberry-dominated forest is the largest heron rookery on the Great Lakes. Black-crowned night herons, great blue herons, great egrets, snowy egrets and cattle egrets are joined by a variety of waterfowl and songbirds.

The fact that it is so inhospitable to humans makes West Sister so irresistible to herons. It is ideal in every way with the glaring exception that there's no food on the island for herons to feed their young. Fortunately, it's within easy distance of the food-filled marshes that lie in virtually all directions of the compass. Adult herons journey to and from the mainland marshes several times each day, a minimum of nine miles one way to Ohio's Lake Erie marshes.

Fishermen are familiar with their sorties. The great blues make regular trips, flapping their huge wings at wave top levels, gaining altitude as they approach the island's rocky ramparts, climbing to clear the treetops. Then it's inland to an unseen nest, invariably a platform of sticks woven so loosely it's a miracle the eggs don't fall through.

The nests may not last long, but the island will. And that's all that really counts.

Great blue herons are common birds of Ohio's wetlands.

Buzzardroost Rock, a promontory of Peebles dolomite, represents the edge of the Appalachian Plateau. There the plateau makes a bold and valiant stand five hundred feet above Ohio Brush Creek before falling off to a wondrously diverse, little-known pocket of Ohio. Some call it Ohio's piece of the Interior Low Plateau, others call it, appropriately, the Edge of Appalachia.

The Edge is second only to the Oak Openings in the size of its family of state-listed endangered plants and animals. Over eighty rare plants and twenty animals can be found in the 11,000 acre Edge of Appalachia Preserve owned and managed by the Cincinnati Museum of Natural History and The Ohio Nature Conservancy.

A red-tailed hawk follows its own scream, bolting ridge-high along highlands splattered in fall color, banking around Buzzardroost, swooping low over the sprawling Edge and on to the valley of the 1,500 acre Ohio Brush Creek Preserve.

It flies over a landscape etched in a geology of dolomites, limestones and shales. Erosion resistant layers of limestone and dolomite make up cliffs, promontories and water-falls, sporting a host of alkaline-loving ferns and flowering plants. Those layers are iced with erosion-prone shales that acid-tolerant plants find to their liking.

By all rights Buzzardroost Rock should be acidic like the ridgetop of which it is a part. But Buzzardroost, once called Split Rock, stands off the end of the ridge, separated by a rocky crevice. The ridge is acidic, Buzzardroost is alkaline.

An oak forest covers the ridge, a postage-stamp-sized prairie dominates Buzzardroost. It's called a promontory prairie, and its small surface supports twenty-one different plant species, thirteen of which are prairie plants, some of them rare. The conditions are extreme. They endure long stretches of hot sun and drying winds without life-giving rainfall. The trade-off is a secure home without competition from woody plants.

Their cousins manage to survive in Lynx Prairie and dozens of other locations, some of the best prairies in the state. There the competition is more intense; cedars and other trees are constantly working to encroach upon them.

The glaciers never touched this part of Ohio, so the limestones and dolomites were never covered with glacial till. But they did come near, pushing plants from the far north ahead of them. Huge white cedars still thrive in a handful of Edge gorges, some of the few sites other than Clifton Gorge where they survive. The runs that cut the gorges are feeder streams to Ohio Brush Creek, which has created its own magnificent works.

Devil's Icebox, a deep, narrow, earth-cooled opening sporting temperatures well below surrounding areas. Other memorable landmarks at Nelson-Kennedy Ledges near Newbury are Dwarf's Pass and Fat Man's Peril.

At "The Swirl," Brush Creek flows headlong into a limestone cliff that turns it an abrupt ninety degrees, forcing it along the cliff's base. After a short run, the cliff juts out again, forcing the stream to turn another ninety. The stream that began flowing southeast is forced through a hairpin and turned northwest. At its second turn, below twenty-foot cliffs, the limestone bed of the stream gives way to soft shales. There the shallow stream cascades softly over a rock shelf, belying a radical drop-off into a 150 foot diameter pool nearly forty feet deep.

Then, a few feet away the stream exits, resuming its shallow course.